Table of Contents

Introductiion

It may be your dream to live on a smallholding in the countryside, with an acre of land.But if, like so many people, you currently live in a small urban apartment, that dream might feel very far away.The truth is that most of the world's population lives in cities, and the number of city dwellers continues to grow. We can't all be farmers. But that doesn't mean that we can't grow any of our own food; anyone can start a small 'garden' in their apartment. In fact, it's something that everyone should do.

If you want to live more sustainably, growing at least some of your own food is a wonderful place to start. It's a great idea to look out for allotments and community garden schemes in your area, giving access to some food-producing land. And even without such opportunities, you could contact the council or local landowners and start your own scheme. Perhaps you and your neighbours could even club together and create a garden in a common area, or on the roof? In France, the law actually decrees that all new rooftops must be covered either with solar panels or with plants.

Even when these options are not possible, you can still start a small garden in your apartment, where you can begin to take back some control over what you eat.

Why Start A Small Indoor Garden?

Even a small indoor garden can be great for both people and planet; you might be amazed by how much difference even a very small garden can make. Benefits include:

- Reducing the amount of food you buy from damaging mono-crop agriculture.
- Lowering food miles and reducing your carbon footprint.
- Lessening the amount of plastic packaging brought into your home.
- Opportunities to reuse plastic, keeping it from the wider environment and prolonging its usefulness.
- Recycling food waste by composting at home, keeping it from landfill.
- And, of course, producing some food in your own home can also save you money.

Choosing Where to Grow Plants in Your Apartment

There are several important considerations when choosing where to grow your plants.

Think about:

- Where and for how long the location in your apartment gets full sun.
- The proximity to artificial heat-sources, and when these are on.
- The average temperatures in the space throughout the year (and how dramatically these fluctuate).
- Ventilation: is the spot very stuffy, or can you create a good breeze
- Accessibility: how easy it will be to reach and maintain your plants.

A light, bright location is best, though many plants prefer not to be in direct sunlight all day long. Try to choose a spot that isn't too close to a heat source like a stove, radiator, or oven, or where temperatures will rise and fall suddenly and dramatically.A little natural ventilation is ideal (ie, where windows can be opened to create a through-breeze). Finally, consider practicality; you need to be able to get to your plants easily to tend and water them, and their containers shouldn't impede other activities within your home.

Maximising the Number of Plants You Can Grow Indoors

When considering how much to grow and where to grow it, it is also important to think about options for maximising growing-space, and which growing systems to use.Often, even in a very small apartment, you can grow a surprising amount of food by considering the following approaches:

Windowsill Gardens

This is the simplest, most traditional way to grow food indoors. Window boxes or other small containers can be placed on inside sills, and (depending on regulations where you live) window boxes can potentially be affixed on the outside of your windows, too.

A south-facing windowsill will offer the best light levels and conditions, but you can grow some plants at a window facing any direction. North-facing windows will get less light, but there are a number of shade-tolerant plants that will still grow.

Placing containers on the existing sill is the easiest way to get started, but you could also dramatically increase your growing area by affixing shelves across a window, or with a narrow shelving unit placed on the windowsill to hold more plants.

Vertical Gardens

Inside or out, this approach is all about thinking vertically to make the most of the space. You might not think you have any space for container plants, but have you considered the vertical space: up walls, and above other interior features?

Shelving is the simplest form of vertical gardening, and doesn't even require DIY. Whether placed in a window or against a sunny wall in your room, you can use any old shelving to increase the amount of container plants in your space.

But shelving isn't the only option; other vertical gardening solutions include:

- Growing plants in pockets (for example, in a fabric shoe-organiser hung on a wall or even a door).
- Creating a tower or vertical structure into which plants can be placed. (For example, a planting tower made from old plastic drinks bottles.)

- A structure in which to grow your plants made from, for example, old plastic plumbing pipes or guttering.
- Climbing plants grown up trellis or supports against a sunny wall, from containers at the base.

These are only a few innovative ways to make use of the vertical space in a room when horizontal space is limited.

Hanging Gardens

Another way to take advantage of the whole room is to utilise ceiling space. Hanging baskets may drip, but plenty of other leak-free containers could be hung inside to grow medium-sized plants securely. Some indoor gardeners simply hang one or two containers on wall or ceiling hooks, while others have even strung multiple containers like bunting along wire or string.

Larger Containers in a Sunny Spot

You may think that you are restricted to small containers inside your apartment. But with a well thought out layout, you may be able to place much larger containers in a sunny spot. By using something like an old 55 gallon barrel, you could create a larger planting area for crops like potatoes that typically need a large area. Holes cut in the container's sides, lined with sacking or similar, can even be used to grow an additional crop like herbs or strawberries.

What Can You Grow Indoors?

You might be surprised by the sheer variety of plants that can be grown in suitable spots within your apartment; you'll only be limited by:

- How much space is available. (Is it just a windowsill, a sunny wall, or an entire spare room, for example?)
- How much time you have to tend your garden. (An indoor garden will be a little more high maintenance than one outside, as crops will all require hand-watering. Certain crops may even need to be hand-pollinated.)

With a little effort and ingenuity, almost any outdoor plants can be grown inside – from certain dwarf fruit trees, to micro-greens and salad crops. However, if you are new to gardening, certain options will be easier than others – for example, the following can be grown in even the smallest of indoors gardens:

- Cut-and-come-again loose-leaf lettuces.
- Brassicas for micro greens
- Cress

- Pea shoots

- Spinach and chard

- Asian greens like pak choi, mizuna, and mibuna

- Radishes

- Spring onions

- Strawberries

- Herbs like basil, mint, rosemary, and thyme.

Once you get the hang of indoors gardening, you could progress to growing:

- Tomatoes

- Peppers (bell peppers and chillies)

- Carrots, beetroots, and other root crops (in deeper window box containers)

- Peas, beans, and other plants that require supports

- Potatoes (in grow-sacks or larger indoor containers or barrels).

- From there, you can branch out to grow a wide range of further produce.

Selecting Containers for a Small Garden Indoors

One of the great things about a small indoors garden is that you can get started cheaply. You do not need to buy containers for planting; instead, consider:

- Using toilet roll tubes or other waste materials (eggshells, newspaper, or other scrap paper folded into small pots) to start your seeds.

- Using clear plastic to create makeshift propagators. Clear plastic trays, tubs, or bags used for food packaging can be placed over seed trays or pots to give a little extra heat when germinating seeds.

- Using food packaging, like yoghurt pots and plastic trays, as plant pots and drip catchers.

- Using old plastic drinks bottles as containers.

- Re-using old kitchen equipment or other upcycled items as containers.

- Upcycling old items of furniture or wood pallets to make shelves or vertical garden structures.

- Sourcing old tools, containers, and growing items for free (or cheap) online.

Creating Compost to Fill Your Containers

While you may initially need to buy some compost (making sure to choose a peat-free option, so as not to deplete peat bog habitats), even in a small apartment, over time you can save money by making your own compost for free.

You can use a small receptacle to compost kitchen waste such as fruit and vegetable scraps, as well as cardboard, paper and other compostable waste. Such a receptacle can easily fit under your kitchen sink, or in another kitchen cabinet out of the way.

You could even speed up the composting process by creating a small compost tumbler, by employing worms in a small-scale vermiculture composter, or by using a bokashi bucket system. Even in a tiny studio apartment, these are all possibilities.

Using Water to Grow Plants Indoors (Small-Scale Hydroponics)

Whether or not you make your own compost, you could also consider growing plants without any soil or compost at all; growing plants in water is a potential small-scale solution for apartment-dwelling food producers. In a simple hydroponics system, plants are floated on rafts with their roots suspended in a container of water. Check out five gallon bucket hydroponics online to see how this can be achieved even in a small apartment.

Harvesting Rainwater for an Apartment Garden

Even in an apartment, it is a good idea to consider whether you can harvest rainwater to water your small garden rather than using water from your tap. Tap water is not as good for plants as rainwater, having less nutriment, and of course it is more sustainable to make use of rainwater if you can.

If possible, discuss installing a rainwater harvesting system for your block, perhaps with your neighbours; you may be able to organise a rainwater harvesting tank on a roof or balcony. Even where this is not possible, a simple alternative is to hang a small bucket or other receptacle out of your window, or place one in a communal outdoor area and use the water collected for your plants.

These things may not be viable where you live, but if you can't harvest rainwater, leave tap water out overnight before using it to water your plants.

Making Liquid Feeds for Container Plants

So, you've got your small apartment garden up and running. Your plants are growing nicely and your watering and compost-creating regimes are sorted. One other thing to consider is how to keep plants healthy in the long term.

Container-grown plants can quickly use up the nutrients in their soil, so will often do better if given a boost during the growing season. Sometimes, adding a little more compost around the top of their containers, or re-potting, will do the trick. But the easiest way to increase vitality is with liquid plant feeds.

The good news is that you can make these quickly and easily at home; options include:

- Making a compost liquid feed by simply diluting some of your home-made compost in water, or taking the run-off from a wormery.
- Make a liquid feed using green teas, or other ingredients (molasses, baking powder, Epsom salts, etc.)
- Harvesting local weeds (like nettles) to make a nitrogen rich liquid feed. The weeds are simply placed into a bucket, covered with water and left to stew for at least six weeks. The plant material rots down and can then be strained, watered down 1:3 (one part nettle brew to three parts water) and used to water your plants.

- Foraging for seaweed on a local beach, or organic matter from a local park (comfrey leaves, for example), to make a liquid feed rich in potassium and micro-nutrients.

Pollinating Indoor Plants by Hand

One final consideration is that an indoor garden will not be accessible by insects – leading to patchy pollination. While some plants are self-pollinating, those usually pollinated by bees and other insects, or by the wind, may require your agency. Where this is the case, simply use a small brush to transfer pollen from one flower to another.

Creating a small garden in your apartment has its challenges – but, over all, getting started is easier, cheaper, and less time consuming than many people imagine. So stop making excuses! Do your part for planet and people by growing at least some of your own food, no matter where you live.

Best Indoor Garden Ideas for Bringing the Great Outdoors Inside

Vegetable gardens, patio planters, and flower beds undoubtedly add appeal to any home and make for some really fun hobbies. But sometimes you just don't have the space, or you might prefer to spend your time inside where the elements (and bugs!) can't really get to you. In these instances, you can never go wrong with curating your own indoor garden.

Lucky for you, the options for indoor gardens are never ending. You can cultivate your own indoor lemon tree, start a delicious herb garden, grow a living wall—or, if you'd rather start simple, try nurturing a small collection of succulents. What makes the indoor version of a garden so fun is how easy it is to mix and match the most random and diverse group of plants and the ability for you to keep your garden blooming and sprouting year-round.

To bring some greenery into your home and experience all the benefits different plants and flowers have to offer, see the ideas below to get started on your own indoor garden.

1. Similarly Sized Collection

Use a small cluster of mid-sized plants, like the ones in this Oakland home, to help take up awkward blank space. Their medium size makes a bigger impact than a small succulent display, but these plants aren't as high maintenance—or difficult to move around—as large indoor trees.

2. Outdoor-Indoor Hybrid Garden

A half-and-half garden helps blend the inside and out, making your home feel even bigger. This colorful home in Mexico is the perfect example of how to make both an indoor and outdoor garden work with your style.

3. Eclectic Indoor Garden

Mixing and matching plants and pots, like the residents of this vintage Australian home did, makes for a visually interesting display for anywhere in your home. Old canisters, handmade pots, and antique finds all work well together.

4. Hanging Herb Garden

Your dinners will seem even tastier with a fresh herb garden at your fingertips. A hanging setup like this means you don't even have to sacrifice any counter space to grow a small collection of herbs.

5. Indoor Garden Closet

Commandeer a set of shelves or closet for your indoor garden, as seen in this plant-laden Brooklyn apartment. If you already have enough storage space for clothes, what better way to deck out an empty nook than with plants?

6. Small Terrarium Garden

An indoor garden doesn't need to be over-the-top or take up ample space, as proven by this terrarium in a comfy Austin home. A few glass display cases and a handful of your favorite air plants or succulents is all it takes to form a mini plant world.

7. Colorful Hanging Garden

One bonus to indoor planting? The ease of mounting planters from the ceiling to create a hanging garden. This maximalist Chicago home shows how colorful plant hammocks and a variety of leafy friends can make a fun statement in any room.

8. Mini Succulent Garden

If you have a tiny empty corner, you have room for an indoor garden. The owners of this Scandinavian-inspired Airstream trailer created a mini succulent collection that still adds a boost of greenery but takes up little room in their small home.

9. Floating Shelf Garden

Floating shelves let you display plants from floor to ceiling, as seen in this Brooklyn apartment. You can place plants based on their light preferences, or even rotate them as needed to keep them healthy.

10. Unique Indoor Garden

For a splash of personality and color, arrange your plants around and inside your non-working or faux fireplace like the tenants of this San Francisco apartment did. You can do this with working fireplaces, too, as long as they're not getting use—so it's a great display for warm spring and summer months, when the fireplace won't be lit.

11. Indoor Greenhouse

As seen in this Nashville home, adding a few fronds and leaves to a mudroom or laundry room space instantly gives it greenhouse vibes. The plants help enliven these utilitarian spaces, adding interest to a room that doesn't always get a lot of love.

12. Kitchen Garden

While herbs are popular for kitchen gardens, they're by no means the only plants that can thrive in your cook space. The residents from the same San Fransisco home from above also allowed plants to take up room in their kitchen for a lively, fresh display.

13. Bathroom Indoor Garden

Convinced you have, like, zero room for an indoor garden? This Philadelphia row home will make you think twice. Your bathroom can be a glorious location for plants, whether you stack a few on a shelf, hang one from the ceiling, or drape one from the shower head (or all the above).

14. Indoor Cactus Garden

Terracotta pots and cacti are a simple but striking display when wall-mounted in cutout shelves, like in this poppy RV home.You could DIY your own version with wood boards and a jig saw.

15. Wall of Plant Cuttings

If you're in full plant parent mode and have started to amass cuttings of your favorite plants, take a cue from this Charleston home and hang them in a chic wall display until they're ready to be repotted.

Benefits of Having a Balcony Garden in an Apartment

Balcony gardens are the much-needed touch of greenery amidst the modern concrete jungle. A balcony garden is very much pleasing to the eyes as well as offers some amazing benefits for apartment dwellers.

Below listed are 5 benefits of having a balcony garden in an apartment.

1. Connect with Nature

Balcony gardens are for those who love the feel of nature in their home. From vertical gardens to potted plants to creepers to hanging plants, options are in abundance to set up a perfect balcony garden and to relax and unwind in the company of nature.

2. Ambience

A touch of greenery in your apartment make the interiors highly appealing and also induces a refreshing feel. Not to mention, having flowering plants or greens adds to the magical charm.

3. Healthy living

A balcony garden acts as a filter for the stale and polluted air entering the apartment and encourages the flow of fresh air which benefits healthy living.

4. Fresh produce

Growing a balcony garden will provide access to fresh produce even if in small quantities. It can be the go-to source for herbs and vegetables like tomatoes, chillies, beans etc.

5. Gardening

For those who hail gardening as their favourite hobby, a balcony garden is the ideal option to encourage their green thumb.

Featuring exclusive balcony gardens for all apartments, Melonwood Greens, flagship project of Melonwood Homes upholds the principle of living with nature in the heart of the city.

Indoor Gardening Pros And Cons

The benefits of gardening indoors are many, especially if that's the only place you have to garden. But those partaking in indoor gardening may find gardening success harder to attain than in an outdoor setting. So, before you think about gardening in your pajamas, take a moment to learn about the disadvantages of indoor gardening and decide for yourself.

Indoor Gardening Pros

If given the option, most plants would probably choose to grow outdoors, where the sunlight is plentiful and there's room to spread out. But it's not up to the plants – it's up to you! And if your outdoor gardening space is limited or nonexistent, indoor gardening is the way to go. Even if you do have the space, there are plenty of advantages of indoor gardening when it comes to controlling the climate and pest protection.

Necessity and flexibility. The most prominent of reasons to grow plants indoors is necessity. While we may dream of expansive gardens, many of us live in houses or apartments with little to no outdoor space. But this doesn't mean we can't flex our green thumbs. You'd be surprised how many plants you can fit in a small space, especially if you're willing to build up. Hanging baskets, shelves, and wall-mounted containers can utilize a small, sunny space to the maximum. Does your house not get enough natural light? A very small investment of a couple grow lights and an outlet timer will simulate a day's worth of outdoor light sun very effectively.

Less pest or disease issues. There are some benefits of gardening indoors that really set it apart from outdoor gardens. One of the most obvious advantages of indoor gardening is protection from pests. While outdoor plants can fall prey to anything and everything from deer to slugs, indoor gardens have built in and very effective protection. The same goes for weed seeds and soil or airborne diseases. Indoor gardens may not be totally pest and disease free, but you do have a lot more control over what can get to them.

You control the environment. Need more reasons to grow plants indoors? Just like the control you have over pests and diseases, your indoor garden will be much less susceptible to the whims of Mother Nature. If a growing season is too wet or too dry, too hot or too cold, your plants won't know any better. And if you have a particularly short growing season, your indoor plants won't mind. With the right treatment, you can grow winter tomatoes in Canada!

Indoor Gardening Cons

The concept of indoor gardening may seem like a very attractive one when we envision growing bountiful plants and produce without ever setting foot outdoors. We may be inclined to think that gardening indoors is easier than growing outdoors, as we would not be subject to Mother Nature's whims and would have more control of the growing environment. The truth is that indoor gardening comes with its own unique challenges and obstacles.

Pet problems. Your beloved pets can wreak havoc on your houseplants either by munching on the leaves or – and this is one of the biggest pitfalls of gardening indoors – by using the plant's soil as a litterbox. Eww! In addition, many plants are toxic to our feline and canine friends. This greatly limits what plants you can grow in your home and the places you situate them in. Your options are much more diverse outdoors without the worry of harming your furry friends inside.

Pestilence and disease. Okay, perhaps they may be somewhat fewer BUT insect populations that take reign on indoor plants, such as aphids, whiteflies and mealybugs, are harder to contain and control due to the lack of biological controls, such as predatory insects, which help keep these detrimental insects at bay. Plant diseases can also take hold if environmental conditions are awry, such as poor air circulation, overwatering, high humidity, etc. – all of which are harder to control in an indoor setting.

Environmental concerns. You may not have to contend with Mother Nature's fury, but when growing plants indoors, it may be difficult to meet and maintain all of their environmental needs. Space, lighting, temperature and humidity must all be considered. These considerations will either make growing certain plants in your home an impossibility or make them high maintenance for you. It may even adversely impact your wallet as certain additional items, such as nutrient solutions, grow lights and fans, may be necessary to foster the environmental requirements for successful growth. This is just another of many indoor gardening cons.

More housework. Do you like additional housework? Yeah, me neither. Well, it's just another one of the disadvantages of indoor gardening. Indoor houseplants require a routine gentle dusting or cleaning in order to look and grow better. Dust accumulates and blocks sunlight, hindering photosynthesis which, in turn, stresses the plant and makes it more vulnerable to pests and diseases.

Disappointed taste buds. Need more reasons against indoor gardening? While taste is unique and subjective to every individual, the debate does exist on whether indoor grown vegetables match the flavor or quality of their outdoor counterparts. While you may be growing winter tomatoes inside, the flavor depends on many variables, such as the amount of sun, nutrient type and water quality. Sunlight, in particular, can make a big difference in terms of boosting flavor and even augmenting plant yields. While there are many lighting options available for indoor gardens, it is probably safe to say that nothing compares to the intensity and benefit of bona fide sunlight.

How Reasons against Indoor Gardening Compare to its Benefits

The reasons to grow plants indoors are varied, but the benefits are great. Whether you want to outsmart Mother Nature or you just don't have access to her, indoor gardening is a wonderful alternative to its more traditional counterpart. Still, the pitfalls of gardening indoors are many, and you must decide whether to rise and meet these unique challenges and whether you will be content with growing plants from a limited catalogue of choices, since not all plants are ideal for growing indoors without extra accommodations.